RAISING
The Mammal Files

Discovery Channel School
Science Collections

Discovery
CHANNEL
SCHOOL™

1 2 3 4 5 6 7 8 9 10 PO 06 05 04 03 02 00 99

Discovery Communications, Inc., produces high-quality television programming,
interactive media, books, films, and consumer products. Discovery Networks, a division of Discovery
Communications Inc., operates and manages Discovery Channel, TLC, Animal Planet, Discovery Health Channel, and Travel Channel.

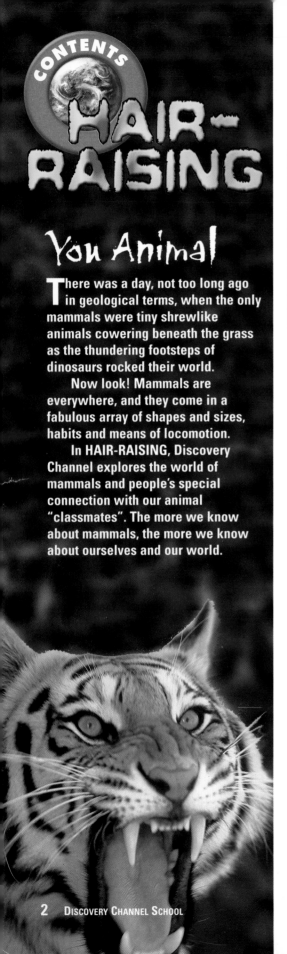

CONTENTS

HAIR-RAISING

You Animal

There was a day, not too long ago in geological terms, when the only mammals were tiny shrewlike animals cowering beneath the grass as the thundering footsteps of dinosaurs rocked their world.

Now look! Mammals are everywhere, and they come in a fabulous array of shapes and sizes, habits and means of locomotion.

In HAIR-RAISING, Discovery Channel explores the world of mammals and people's special connection with our animal "classmates". The more we know about mammals, the more we know about ourselves and our world.

The Mammal Files

See page 7

Final Project

Mammals

Mammals: You know them, you love them, and you're one of them. Humans share the planet with about 4,000 other species of mammals, from the thumb-sized pygmy shrew to the three-times-as-long-as-a-city-bus blue whale.

Not every creature, of course, is a mammal. There are only two entrance requirements: hair, and milk from mammary glands. But most mammals have other features in common too.

FEATURE: DIFFERENTIATED TEETH
Many mammals have teeth designed for a variety of tasks.

FEATURE: BLUBBER
An adaptation unique to polar bears and some other mammals, blubber is layered skin with insulating fat glands (milk, sebaceus, and sweat).

There are three different kinds of mammals:

PLACENTAL—Those nourished inside their mother's uterus through a placenta

MARSUPIAL—Those developed in a uterus but sheltered and fed in their mother's pouch

MONOTREMES—Those developed in eggs

FEATURE: A BACKBONE
You have to have a backbone to be a mammal, but just because you have one doesn't automatically make you a mammal. Fish and frogs have them too.

FEATURE: FOUR LIMBS
You can have two legs and two arms, four legs or a pair of flippers and fins.

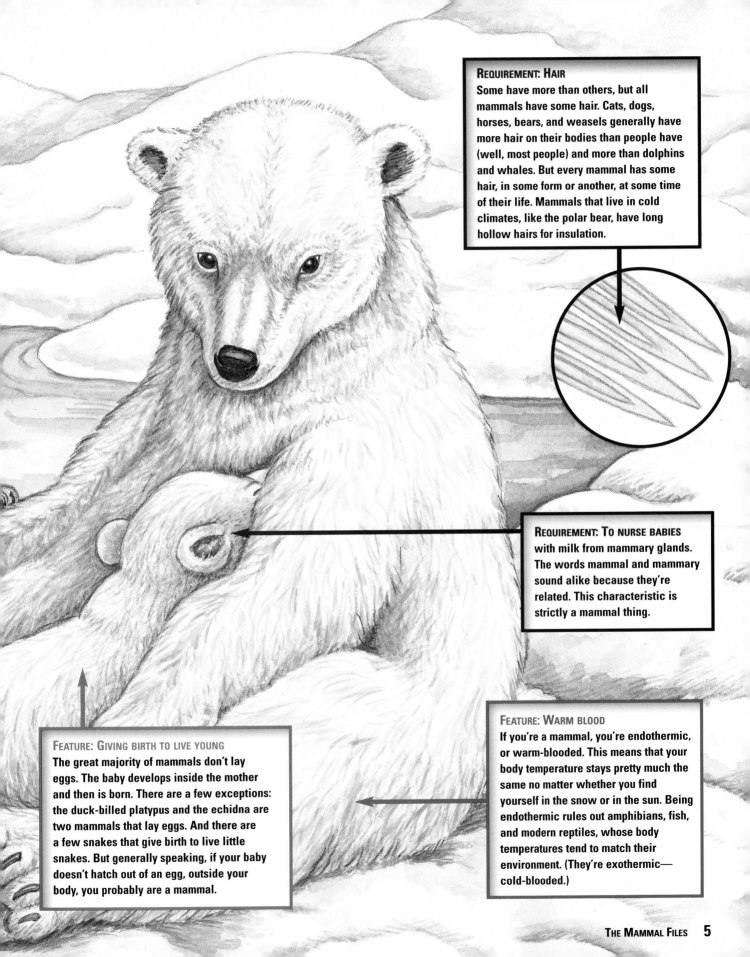

REQUIREMENT: HAIR
Some have more than others, but all mammals have some hair. Cats, dogs, horses, bears, and weasels generally have more hair on their bodies than people have (well, most people) and more than dolphins and whales. But every mammal has some hair, in some form or another, at some time of their life. Mammals that live in cold climates, like the polar bear, have long hollow hairs for insulation.

REQUIREMENT: TO NURSE BABIES
with milk from mammary glands. The words mammal and mammary sound alike because they're related. This characteristic is strictly a mammal thing.

FEATURE: GIVING BIRTH TO LIVE YOUNG
The great majority of mammals don't lay eggs. The baby develops inside the mother and then is born. There are a few exceptions: the duck-billed platypus and the echidna are two mammals that lay eggs. And there are a few snakes that give birth to live little snakes. But generally speaking, if your baby doesn't hatch out of an egg, outside your body, you probably are a mammal.

FEATURE: WARM BLOOD
If you're a mammal, you're endothermic, or warm-blooded. This means that your body temperature stays pretty much the same no matter whether you find yourself in the snow or in the sun. Being endothermic rules out amphibians, fish, and modern reptiles, whose body temperatures tend to match their environment. (They're exothermic—cold-blooded.)

Ch-ch-ch-ch-changes

Over billions of years, our planet has undergone quite a few changes. Environments have cooled down, heated up, gotten wetter, gotten drier. Oceans, deserts, forests, grasslands, tundra, mountains, beaches have come and gone. And with these changes have come new species of animals and plants that have changed, or adapted, to live in these conditions and ecosystems. Mammals have undergone a staggering variety of changes since they first appeared on Earth. How have these changes come about? In the 1800s, there was a great debate about that.

Paris, France, 1809

French scientist Jean-Baptiste Lamarck thought animals changed by using parts to fit into the conditions around them:

It is interesting to observe the result of habit in the peculiar shape and size of the giraffe (Camelo-Pardalis): this animal, the largest of the mammals, is known to live in the interior of Africa in places where the soil is nearly always arid and barren, so that it is obliged to browse on the leaves of trees and to make constant efforts to reach them. From this habit long maintained in all its race, it has resulted that the animal's fore-legs have become longer than its hind legs, and that its neck is lengthened to such a degree that the giraffe, without standing up on its hind legs, attains a height of six metres (nearly 20 feet).

Cambridge, England, 1859

Half a century later, Charles Darwin had a different idea. Darwin argued that animals changed because the environment selected the most successful traits. In other words, giraffes have long necks because those animals with long necks were the ones that survived to reproduce and pass along their long-necked genes:

It may be said that natural selection is daily and hourly scrutinizing, throughout the world, every variation, even the slightest; rejecting that which is bad, preserving and adding up all that is good; silently and insensibly working, whenever and wherever opportunity offers, at the improvement of each organic being in relation to its organic and inorganic conditions of life. We see nothing of these slow changes in progress, until the hand of time has marked the long lapses of ages, and then so imperfect is our view into long past geological ages, that we only see that the forms of life are now different from what they formerly were.

Science confirms that Darwin was right. There are variations within a population, and some of these variations might help an animal survive better and pass along the genes for that particular characteristic. The process is called *natural selection*. It's what drives evolution, the development over time of all living things, incorporating gradual changes. The examples on the next page show how certain animals have adapted.

Take a look at these two foxes, noting their differences. Why is the one on the left suited to the desert, and the one on the right to the north polar regions?

Think this bear is white? Think again. Underneath its fur, the polar bear is black. Black skin soaks up heat from the sun and helps keep the animal warm. The bear appears white because it is covered with white, but hollow, hair. The hollowness helps the polar bear float in water. In what other ways do you think this bear is adapted to its environment?

HIGH FLIERS

Bats are the only mammals that fly. How did these animals get their wings? Bat ancestors lived in trees and ate insects and fruit. Somewhere along the line a bat was born with a flap of skin that stretched across the finger bones. Perhaps this extra skin webbing gave that bat ancestor some sort of advantage and it reproduced and passed the characteristic on to its offspring. After generations and generations of bats, the fingers became very long and a thin membrane joined the fingers together to become wings.

UNDERWATER MAMMALS

Whales, including dolphins, are mammals that spend their lives in water. Their bodies have adapted to underwater life in a number of ways:

- **Bodies** are smooth and streamlined with little hair and no external ears.
- **Limbs** are strong, rigid fins and flukes that help them swim.
- A layer of blubber beneath the skin insulates them like a wet suit from the cold waters they live in.

Activity

START YOUR OWN SCRAPBOOK How have other mammals adapted for life today? Make an adaptation scrapbook. Cut out pictures of mammals and the environments they live in and make notes about why these animals look the way they do. Do their looks have anything to do with how they related to their environment? Fill your scrapbook with pictures, articles, notes, and drawings.

GROWING UP

Did you know you're related to a lizard? No, not your cousin Harold. Scientists believe mammals evolved from a group of reptilelike animals called synapsids, which lived 320–275 million years ago. Mammals developed and adapted to a changing environment over millions and millions of years from scaly creeping things to the furry selves of all sorts we know today.

The development of mammals took more than just time: it took a lucky break. When this planet was ruled by enormous dinosaurs, there wasn't a lot of room for a little mammal to survive and be happy. The mammals that did exist were tiny and shy.

But then something drastic occurred to kill the dinosaurs. Many scientists believe that a huge asteroid struck the earth, sending up clouds of dust into the air. That killed the plants that were the plant-eating dinosaurs' food source. The meat-eating dinosaurs whose main meals were the plant-eaters couldn't survive. But the little mammals that fed on meat had plenty to eat: all the dinosaurs. They found a way to survive and reproduce. NOW look. Mammals are everywhere.

3,500 MILLION YEARS AGO	**500 MILLION YEARS AGO**	**360 MILLION YEARS AGO**	**AROUND 320 MILLION YEARS AGO**	**AROUND 286 MILLION YEARS AGO**	**AROUND 213 MILLION YEARS AGO**
Life is just beginning to form in the seas.	Snails and other simple animals such as sponges and sea-jellies show up.	The first amphibians appear.	Synapsids, with jaws and teeth, appear. These animals will give rise to mammals.	The first reptiles appear.	The first dinosaurs begin to roam the earth. They will rule for over 125 million years.

MAMMAL

AROUND 160 MILLION YEARS AGO	AROUND 130 MILLION YEARS AGO	AROUND 65 MILLION YEARS AGO	AROUND 14 MILLION YEARS AGO	AROUND 4 MILLION YEARS AGO	TODAY
The first furry animals with sharp teeth and four legs appear: the first mammals. They're tiny and look like a tree shrew.	The dinosaurs rule the earth. Mammals such as the insect-eating *Morganucodontis* continue to thrive in the underbrush.	The dinosaurs mysteriously die out, leaving room for the mammals to take over.	Some mammals are huge! Giant creatures such as the *Indricotherium*, a hornless rhinoceros and the largest land mammal ever, wander the earth.	Hominids, ancestors of modern humans, appear on the scene.	Mammals of many shapes and sizes walk, swim, or fly around Earth.

Activity

MAMMAL MILLENNIA Pick a mammal, any mammal, and be a time detective. Do a little digging and find out how that mammal evolved. Pick five stages of evolutionary development and make a drawing of each stage. Under each picture write when and where the mammal lived and how it changed. End with how the mammal looks today and how it has evolved to fit the environment in which it is found.

ORDER,

All mammals have hair and nurse their young with milk. But this hardly describes the great diversity between a tree shrew, an elephant, a spiny anteater, and a rhinoceros. Since their first appearance in the Triassic Period, mammals have evolved into a wide range of spectacular and not-so-spectacular animals.

The simplest way to think about the classification of mammals is to divide them into monotremes (duck-billed platypus), marsupials (pouched animals), and placental animals (all other living mammals). Since mammalogists find this system a bit inaccurate, it might be easier to think of all living mammals as belonging to 21 orders. These orders are shown on the right. Classification is not a foolproof system, though, and is always subject to change. New knowledge, or a reinterpretation of old data, may further refine this system of classification. But despite what names scientists assign to them, mammals are an amazing assortment of animals.

Classification Chart

Order	Common Name
Monotremata	One hole
Marsupialia	**With a pouch**
Artiodactyla	Even-toed
Carnivora	**Flesh-eating**
Cetacea	Like whales
Chiroptera	**Hand wing**
Dermoptera	Skin wing
Endentata	**Toothless**
Hyracordea	Like hyraxes
Insectivora	**Insect-eating**
Lagomorpha	Rabbit-shaped
Macroscelia	**Large legs**
Perissodactyla	Odd-toed
Pholidata	**Scaly ones**
Pinnipedia	Fin feet
Primates	**First**
Proboscidea	Trunk-nosed
Rodentia	**Like rodents**
Sirenia	Like sirens
Tubulidentata	**Tubular teeth**
Xenarthra	Unusual joints

PLEASE

The Orders of Mammals

Examples	Characteristics
Platypus, spiny anteater	Lay eggs instead of giving birth to live young
Kangaroo, koala, opossum	**Immature offspring reared in abdominal pouch**
Sheep, pig, giraffe, deer, cattle, camel	Herbivores; hooves with two or four toes
Cat, wolf, otter, weasel, bear	**Large canine teeth, clawed feet; many hunt and kill**
Whale, dolphin, porpoise	Aquatic; blowholes on top of head, front flippers
Bat	**Only flying mammals; navigate by echolocation**
Flying lemur	Fangs and wide incisors; glide from tree to tree
Anteater	**Lacking teeth or small simple teeth; eat mostly insects**
Hyrax	Herbivores; hooves and teeth like rhinoceroses
Mole, shrew, hedgehog	**Small with long snout, sharp cusped teeth**
Rabbit, hare, pika	Four upper incisors; hind legs adapted for jumping
Elephant shrew	**Shrewlike appearance with elongated noses and large back legs**
Horse, zebra, tapir, rhinoceros	Herbivores; hooves with one or three toes
Pangolin	**Covered with horny scales; eat ants and termites**
Seal, sea lion, walrus	Marine carnivores; modified limbs for swimming
Human, monkey, ape	**Large brains; opposable thumbs; binocular vision**
African and Asian elephants	Large herbivores; trunks, elongated trunks
Mouse, rat, beaver, squirrel	**Small herbivores with chisel-like incisors**
Dugong, manatee	No back legs; front flippers; eat water plants in estuaries
Aardvark	**Dig up termites for food; have only four or five peglike teeth**
Sloth, armadillo	Sloths are arboreal; armadillos have scale-like covering

Activity

CLASSIFY IT Most of us can report on the biology of cats or dogs, mammals we are familiar with. But what do you know of the dugong, the elephant shrew, the pangolin, or the tapir? Scan the examples column above and pick one animal that you know little or nothing about. Prepare a report on the biology of this mammal: its distribution, habit, ecology, and all other aspects of its life. Share your information with the class.

The MAMMAL HALL of FAME

ALMANAC

Compare a walrus to a weasel … a leopard to a llama … a person to a pig. What's the unavoidable conclusion? Mammals are full of diversity. Here are some record-setters.

LONGEST JUMPER

Kangaroos can leap up to 30 feet (9 m) in one bound.

BIGGEST MAMMAL—The blue whale, which can grow up to 100 feet (30 m) long and weigh up to 100 tons—a ton a foot! It's not only the biggest mammal, it's the biggest creature that ever lived. Even the biggest dinosaur, Brachiosaurus, was only 74 feet (23 m) long. This mighty mammal of the deep eats tiny shrimplike animals called krill. But it eats a LOT of them.

Smallest Mammal

The smallest mammal is the pygmy shrew, which measures less than two inches (5 cm) long, minus its tail. The tiny shrew is an eating machine. It burns up food so fast that if it stopped eating for half a day it would die of starvation.

SLOWEST-MOVING MAMMAL

The sloth from South America. It moves about half a mile (.8 km) a day. Spending its entire life in the trees, the sloth hangs upside down by its hook-shaped claws, grazing on leaves. Some appear green because their hair is the perfect mobile home for algae.

FLYING MAMMALS

Bats are the only mammals that can actually fly from place to place. Flying squirrels glide with the help of loose skin flaps along the sides of their bodies.

MAMMAL WITH THE LONGEST HAIR

You! Human beings win this category. If you didn't cut your hair, it would reach the floor. This goes for beards and mustaches, too. After hairy humans, musk oxen run a close second.

SWIMMING MAMMALS

Marine mammals are mammals that live in the ocean. Whales (including dolphins and porpoises) and seals are all mammals. They breathe air, but they live their lives in the water.

HIGHEST JUMPER

The puma can leap straight up to 20 feet (6 m) from standing.

TALLEST MAMMAL

The giraffe. An adult male giraffe can reach 18 feet (5.5 m), or three times the height of a tall human male. Amazingly, the giraffe's neck has the same number of neck bones as you do—seven. Each one is just a lot longer. Its neck allows it to reach the tender leaves of the tallest trees, which are beyond the reach of any other herbivore.

BIGGEST LAND MAMMAL

African elephant, which can grow up to 11 feet (3.4 m) high and weigh 17,000 pounds (7,711 kg).

Activity

CLAIM TO FAME Like humans, every animal is special in its own way. Every mammal has something interesting and unique about it. To prove it, pick a letter of the alphabet at random. Then go to an encyclopedia or another source and find a mammal whose name begins with that letter. Do some research and then explain why it should belong in the Hall of Fame. Perhaps your mammal is the best smeller, has the biggest ears, can hold its breath the longest, or has the most teeth. What makes it unique? Combine some library research with firsthand observations and add this information to your journal.

SPOTlight on a PREDATOR

The human body is designed to get energy from meat and plant food sources. We can choose to be vegetarians, but we don't have to be. Nature is more limiting with other mammals. Some mammals eat insects. Some eat plants. And others … well, you know what's left.

Q: You're a cheetah. Love your spots.

A: Thanks. I use 'em every day. They're more than just beauty marks, you know. They help me earn a living.

Q: What do you mean?

A: They let me blend, and blending's a beautiful thing. See, I have to sneak up on prey if I want to eat—and I DO want to eat. When I move through tall grass and brush, my spots look just like shadows in the sunlight. Can't see me coming. I can get up close and … gotcha!

Q: I see. Very impressive. What else do you have to say about yourself?

A: Well, there are my teeth. Come on—take a look. Come closer.

Q: Uh, well, OK. Sure. Hmm … pretty sharp-looking!

A: Yep, and they work as good as they look. Sharp, pointy teeth are great for biting and ripping into flesh. You won't see choppers like these on any old plant-eater. Herbivores have flat teeth to chomp on grasses and grind up leaves. Works for them, but I'm a carnivore. I need meat. It's the only thing my body can use for the kind of energy I need.

Q: Any other special features I should be noticing, as long as I'm still up close? At least, for another minute?

A: My eyes. See how they face forward?

Q: How can I help it? But what does that have to do with anything?

A: Tut, tut. Everything is good for something in nature. My eyes face forward so I can scope out my territory and focus on my prey.

Q: That is interesting. Anything else?

A: Sure. I've been saving the best for last. You've probably heard about how fast I am—in fact, if I were running on most highways, I could get a ticket for speeding. I've been clocked at up to 70 miles per hour (that's 112 kilometers per hour), and I've got the strong, long legs to prove it. Built for speed. Gotta be fast to catch one of those tasty gazelles. They don't exactly dawdle, you know. Can't catch them every time. And they're tricky. They weave back and forth trying to get away.

Q: Well, can you blame them?

A: Course not. They have their job, and I have mine. Predators try to catch prey, and they try to get away. It's all part of the game: Plants make the energy they need from the sun. Herbivores get energy for their bodies from plants. Carnivores get energy from the flesh of these herbivores. They eat grass, we eat them … simple as that. It's the food chain, and it works for me. Of course, I'm close to the top.

Q: Is there an easy way to "spot" a prey animal?

A: The eyes can be a dead giveaway—so to speak. Rabbits, deer, gazelles, zebras and other prey have eyes on the sides of their heads. That gives them an advantage in "spotting" danger, wherever it's coming from.

Q: What other predators are out there?

A: You've got the big cats—lions, leopards, cheetahs, bobcats, mountain lions. And then there's the canine crowd—the dogs like wolves, wild dogs, dingoes, foxes, coyotes, jackals. There are hyenas, weasels, orcas, bears, and seals.

Q: What about us? Human beings?

A: Well, look at your own eyes. Not on the sides of your head, now, are they? What do you think that means? And how about those sharp pointy teeth in the front of your mouth? What do you think they're for, decoration?

Q: Never thought of it that way.

A: Well, I can't blame you. You guys' hunting days are over. You just go to the supermarket, and all the meat there is already dead. But it's no disgrace to be a predator. Actually, we perform a service.

Q: How so?

A: We usually end up catching the weak, old, sick or hurt animals. That way we weed out the weak ones and leave the strong ones to continue and reproduce. So we keep our prey strong, fast, and healthy. And the same is true for us. If we're not up to snuff in the running, hunting, catching departments, dinner is NOT served. We don't eat, and we don't survive. Other predators get our food. So predators and prey depend on each other. We all keep each other going. You can't just remove an animal because you don't like the idea of predators. Speaking of that, I gotta run. I'm starving! See ya!

Activity

PREY TELL The cheetah has its spots for camouflage as it stalks its prey. Pick a habitat such as the East African plain and research some other features of different predators. Write about why they are effective.

NEVER CRY WOLF

Predators and prey are, over time, in a sort of ecological balance. But sometimes the balance can get tipped—or at least, seems to. In 1963, as part of a government wildlife mission, scientist and writer Farley Mowat came to northern Canada to observe Arctic wolves. These predators were supposedly slaughtering an alarmingly high number of caribou. Ranchers feared for the safety of their cattle and sheep.

Mowat moved into a cabin in the wilderness and proceeded to get to know two wolves whose den was nearby. What he found was not what he expected, as this account of his third meeting with them shows.

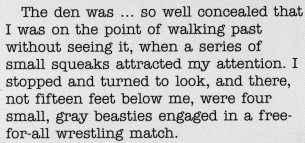

The den was ... so well concealed that I was on the point of walking past without seeing it, when a series of small squeaks attracted my attention. I stopped and turned to look, and there, not fifteen feet below me, were four small, gray beasties engaged in a free-for-all wrestling match.

At first I did not recognize them for what they were. The fat, fox faces with pinprick ears; the butterball bodies, as round as pumpkins; the short, bowed legs and the tiny upthrust sprigs of tails were so far from my conception of a wolf that my brain refused to make the logical connection.

Suddenly one of the pups caught my scent. He stopped in the midst of attempting to bite off a brother's tail and turned smoky blue eyes up toward me. What he saw evidently intrigued him. Lurching free of the scrimmage, he padded toward me with a rolling, wobbly gait; but a flea bit him unexpectedly before he had gone far, and he had to sit down to scratch it.

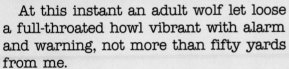

At this instant an adult wolf let loose a full-throated howl vibrant with alarm and warning, not more than fifty yards from me.

The pups became gray streaks which vanished into the gaping darkness of the den mouth. I spun around to face the adult wolf, lost my footing, and started to skid down the loose slope toward the den.... I shot past the den mouth, over the lip of the main ridge and down the full length of the esker slope....

When I got myself straightened out and glanced back up at the esker, it was to see three adult wolves ranged side by side, all peering down at me with expressions of incredulous delight....

On three separate occasions in less than a week I had been completely at the mercy of these "savage killers" but far from attempting to tear me limb from limb, they had displayed a restraint verging on contempt, even when I invaded their home and appeared to be posing a direct threat to the young pups.

Activities

BIG BAD WOLF? Wolves have often been the subject of controversy and debate, and there is more of it now than ever. Naturalists want to reintroduce them to the wild in places like Montana because of deer overpopulation. But ranchers are afraid the wolves will slaughter their cattle or sheep. Do research to examine both sides of this issue and have a class debate. Use discoveryschool.com along with other sites and the library.

MIND OVER MYTH Farley Mowat approached the wolves with an open mind to form his own opinions. How have myths about animals contributed to what we think about them? Take an animal and make a list of words that describe what you think they're like, based on just your own memories and associations. Then do some research about the animal's habits. Make another list and compare the two. Are the myths correct? Start with these: Pigs are dirty. Lions are noble.

LIFE AMONG

For 40 years, British zoologist Jane Goodall has been living with and studying chimpanzees in Gombe, on the shores of Lake Tanganyika in Africa. Chimpanzees are perhaps our nearest relatives in the mammal class, and Goodall has discovered, through observing their communal life, that they are more like humans than anyone thought before. In the following excerpts from her book *Through a Window*, she writes about the behavior of chimpanzees in the Kasakela community—animals to whom Goodall has given names.

Chimpanzees and humans are among the few mammals to use logical thinking to problem-solve. Here Goodall observes Gigi, a female chimp as she solves the problem of feasting on a nest of delicious army ants without getting bitten by them.

Upon arrival at the site she [Gigi] broke a long straight branch from a nearby bush, removed the side branches, then carefully stripped the bark until she had made a smooth tool, about three feet long. She reached her hand a short way into the opening of the nest and, for a few seconds, dug frantically until the ants began to swarm out. Quickly she plunged her tool into the nest, waited for a moment, then withdrew it covered by a seething mass of ants. With rapid movements she swept the stick through her free hand, pushed the ant-mass into her mouth, and crunched vigorously. As the ants poured out of the nest in ever greater numbers, agitated by the intrusion, Gigi climbed a sapling nearby and, reaching down with her stick, continued her meal.

Chimpanzees form strong bonds of love and affection just as humans do. Mothers are extremely close to their children, but so are brothers and sisters, as Goodall observes in the relationship between Wolfi and his elder sister Wunda, after the death of their mother.

Wunda had carried him [Wolfi] frequently when the family travelled, not only because, like all elder sisters, she was fascinated with her small brother, but also because, from the time he was able to totter, Wolfi had wanted to follow her wherever she went. Again and again Wunda had set off about her own concerns, only to return when she heard the sad cries of her small brother as he tried, most desperately, to keep up. Then she would gather him up, and off they would go, together.

THE CHIMPS

But if chimpanzees exhibit the better traits of human beings, they also demonstrate the darker ones. In 1974, the group of chimpanzees split, for no apparent reason, into two sub-groups—the Kasakela and the Kahama. Patrols of adults travelled along the boundaries of their territory and brutally attacked any Kahama chimpanzees they encountered. In this excerpt, six adult Kasakela males come upon a young Kahama male named Godi feeding in a tree.

Humphrey was the first to grab Godi, seizing one of his legs and throwing him to the ground. Figen, Jomeo, Sherry, and Evered pounded and stamped on their victim, while Humphrey pinned him to the ground, sitting on his head and holding his legs with both hands. Godi had no chance to escape, no chance to defend himself. Rodolf, the oldest of the Kasakela males, hit and bit at the hapless victim whenever he saw an opening …. After ten minutes Humphrey let go of Godi. The others stopped their attack and left in a noisy, boisterous group. Godi … was badly wounded, with great gashes on his face, one leg and the right side of his chest, and must have been badly bruised by the tremendous pummelling to which he had been subjected. Undoubtedly he died of his injuries, for he was never seen again by the field staff and students working in the Kahama community range.

Activity

JUST WATCH ME Keep a journal of a mammal, either a pet or another animal. Observe it closely in as many situations as possible. Write about what you see. Try to write something every day. What conclusions can you make about your mammal and the way it relates to other animals like itself—unlike itself—and to humans?

Magnificent Marsupials and Marvelous Monotremes

There are three basic kinds of mammals. Most are placental mammals. That means unborn babies are nourished through a membrane called a placenta. The placenta absorbs oxygen and nutrients from the mother's blood and passes them along to the embryo through the umbilical cord. This is how it happened with you. (Check your belly button for evidence—it's where the umbilical cord was attached to you as a baby.)

But other mammals do the baby thing a little differently. Some lay eggs. They're called monotremes, and there are only a couple of them— the duckbilled platypus and the spiny anteater, or echidna. Once the female lays her eggs, she puts them in a skin flap on her belly until they hatch. After they hatch, the babies stay in the pouch and nurse on milk until they are ready to come out.

Marsupials are the third kind of mammals. They also have a pouch, but they don't lay eggs. Instead, they give birth to tiny embryonic babies about the size of a jellybean. These jellybean babies have to make their way out of the mother's body and into the pouch on their mother's belly and attach themselves to a nipple. They stay there for weeks or months, nursing on milk and growing. When they develop, they are ready to leave the pouch.

Only one kind of marsupial lives in America—the opossum. All the other 259 species of marsupials live in Australia and on the nearby islands of Tasmania and New Guinea.

The echidna, or spiny anteater, is about 15 inches (38 cm) long and covered with spines. The female lays one egg at a time. She deposits it into her skin flap and it hatches and nurses until it has hair. At that point it ventures forth out of the flap.

Duckbilled platypuses have rubbery bills and webbed feet. They also lay eggs. Kind of sounds like a bird, you say? It does. Those are birdlike qualities. But what makes this odd creature a mammal is the fact that it has fur, not feathers, and it nurses its baby with milk. Only mammals nurse their babies with milk.

Numbats are cat-sized marsupials that eat termites. They are covered with both spots and stripes.

Quokkas are marsupial cats.

Tasmanian devils are loud, cranky little meat-eaters. They are about the size of a small dog, with strong jaws and a powerful bite that they use to protect their territories from other animals.

Koalas are covered in soft, gray fur and spend their time in eucalyptus trees. They have a rounded shape, which is no accident. They're round because they have very large intestines, which they need to digest the eucalyptus leaves. Koalas have pouches, but the opening is toward the back.

WHAT'S IN A NAME?

Check out these other wildly named marsupials:

Wombat   Chuditch
Wallaby   Wopilkara
Bandicoot   Djoongary
Cus-cus   Dibbler

NOT ALONE IN THE DARK

The sun has just gone down. You have special glasses to help you see at night. You're cramped in this small, dark place, but you're not alone.

There are bats everywhere: flying in and out of the entrance, hanging upside down from the cave ceiling, crouching on the cave floor. But the funny thing is that they don't seem to be making any noise. Except for the rustle of their wings flying past your ear you can't hear anything.

The other odd thing is that even though it's dark, and there are hundreds of bats flying around the cave, none of them has an accident. Watch out! A bat is heading right for you! But at the last second it steers clear.

You wouldn't know it, but the bats are making noises constantly. They make a kind of high-pitched squeak—too high for people to hear—that allows them to "see" in the dark. This helps them fly at night and catch insects to eat. Called echolocation, this ability works a lot like radar.

Like all sounds, the bat's chirping has an echo. The sound goes out and then bounces against something such as an insect. This echo is a signal to the bat, telling it exactly where the insect is. Good-bye insect! Do you notice how few insects, blackflies, and midges there are in this cave? That's because the bats have eaten so many of them.

Bats have to catch and kill roughly half their own body weight in bugs to have enough to eat. They catch the insects as they fly and then flip the bugs into their tail membrane to eat later. Don't step on those other live insects you see at your feet—those are for dinner.

Watch your head—there's a mother nursing her baby. She's got a heavy load: at birth, the baby is already a quarter of her own weight. Luckily, her milk is extra-rich, which helps the baby grow quickly. The one you're holding in your hand isn't yet full grown, but it's ready to fly.

DO NOT DISTURB

If it were winter, you'd see thousands of bats hanging upside down on the ceiling, sound asleep. They grip the cave roof with their toe claws and wrap their wings around them like a blanket.

Hibernation is how some bats survive when their food supply is scarce. Their body temperature plunges and their heartbeat slows down to 8 pulses per minute. Bats can burn as much as 80 percent of their body fat during hibernation. So don't disturb a hibernating bat: just the act of waking up can cause the bat to burn a few weeks' supply of energy —enough to prevent it from surviving the winter.

Activity

FAT INSULATES Fat and fur are a mammal's key to surviving the cold winter. Whether or not a mammal hibernates, it's still important to maintain a constant body temperature. Try this. Take two glasses of warm water and wrap one with a towel. Secure the towel with a rubber band and place both glasses in the refrigerator for an hour. Check the temperature of the water. Dip your fingers into each glass. Which is warmer? Why?

Mammal or Not?

Africa, Present Time

The late afternoon sun is hot and the heat shimmers up from the African desert sands, making the huge termite mounds seem to jiggle and sway. Night is beginning to fall, bringing a hint of coolness. Nocturnal animals begin to stir. Inside the mound, the termite queen is busy laying eggs while the worker insects bustle around her bringing food, caring for the eggs, or making the nest strong and safe.

Nearby, you stop. There is something moving underground. Using your sensitive audio equipment, you scan the sand. Your equipment picks up a series of digging sounds as well as clicks, squeaks and high-pitched grunts.

Quickly you dig down deep into the sand and you are rewarded. An odd-looking, pink, soft, wrinkly animal with a few prickly hairs writhes and waves its four legs in the air. Its skin is so loose that the animal can twist around inside it. Sharp claws almost cut you. This creature is strong! And it has sharp-looking mouth parts.

You release it and it digs into the sand. Slowly you uncover the intricate burrow. Tunnels are filled with these creatures that seem to move easily both forward and backward.

One is larger than the rest—and it is a female. She is giving birth. Tiny pink creatures wriggle free of her as you watch, then make their way to a nipple to nurse. The others take care of the babies, bring the mother food and dig.

Examining a couple of creatures, you discover they have a low body temperature. Their temperature exactly matches the temperature of the burrow.

After you've finished scribbling your notes, you replace the sand and head back to camp, eager to figure out exactly what kind of animal this is.

Classifying animals is a way to organize the different species. Each kind of animal group has certain characteristics, but sometimes the lines blur. Your mystery animal shares qualities of many animals. Based on your observations and the information in the clue envelope, determine what kind of animal you've discovered.

Clues

INSECTS	MAMMALS
• Some species live in complex social groups	• Hair
• Sometimes have a queen that is the only female to produce young	• Endothermic—regulate body heat so their temperature generally stays the same no matter the environment
• Some other insects are workers	• Give birth to live young
• Exothermic—same temperature as surroundings	• Feed milk to babies
• No backbone	• Backbone
• Six legs	• Four legs
• Three body-segments	

No Offense, but You Really Smell

Human beings have five senses, and they work pretty well to help us figure out the world around us. But those senses work even better in other mammals. Wild and domestic cats have better vision. Bats have better hearing. And when it comes to sniff power, nobody can beat a bloodhound. It's the winner by a lot more than a nose. It can sniff you out from the tiniest trace—a hair clip, a shoelace. Even when you can't smell yourself, a bloodhound can. In fact, to a bloodhound, you reek. And that's a good thing. Bloodhounds are used in rescue work all over the world. They've located countless missing children and adults, even when human searchers have given up. To loving friends and families, bloodhounds are true heroes.

But what makes their sense of smell so superior?

First, you have to understand that mammals smell with the use of their olfactory (ohl-FAC-tory) cells. These are located in the nose, making up tissue called the olfactory membrane. A bloodhound's snout is much bigger than the average person's nose. And so its olfactory membrane, covering 150 square centimeters, is 50 times bigger than ours. Compared to a bloodhound, we can hardly smell anything at all.

Bloodhounds don't "forget" a scent, either. You can walk into a kitchen and get a strong whiff of frying sausages, and a few minutes later you won't notice the odor anymore. Your nose gets used to the smell. This is because of a powerful built-in odor block that humans have. Once we sense that something in our surroundings isn't a threat, we no longer notice it. But bloodhounds don't have this odor-blocking ability. For them, scents stay strong. On the trail, bloodhounds also keep their olfactory cells fresh by taking quick sniffs and then emptying their noses to give the olfactory cells a rest.

Another special feature bloodhounds have are their highly-tuned receptor sites. These "lock on" to a certain scent, helping the hound identify it and stay with it. Bloodhounds happen to have lots of receptor sites that are specially tuned to human scents.

So what does a bloodhound smell, anyway, when he's hot on your trail? Well, your cells. They come off you in tiny pieces of skin and fall to the ground. "Invisible dandruff" is the way these bits are described by Hilda Onderdonk, who, with her husband, David, owns two bloodhounds and regularly helps in rescue work. "If there's any breeze, it'll get blown away. But sooner or later it gets caught in the grass or the bushes. This is a scent pattern, the way it falls, and a bloodhound trails that scent."

Believe it or not, you shed 50 million cells a day, along with plenty of sweat. Skin and sweat don't have much of a smell, but the bacteria on them do. They give you your own scent, which is as distinctive as a fingerprint. Even identical twins don't have the same scent.

To prove this, David Onderdonk did an experiment with a pair of identical twin girls. These two were so much alike that as babies they had to go back to the

hospital several times so that their names could be checked against their footprint records. Their own parents finally insisted that one girl wear her hair short and the other long, just so they could be told apart.

The two girls walked across a golf course that had been used by golf players all day. The long-haired twin went to the left and hid. Mr. Onderdonk gave one of the bloodhounds her nightshirt to smell. Instantly the dog dashed across the golf course, following the girl's trail perfectly. He found her without missing a beat.

Some scientists say that all that loose skin on a bloodhound's neck helps it follow a scent. As the dog puts its nose to the ground, the skin falls forward. This creates a cupping effect (see picture, above) that traps the smell for the dog and makes it even stronger. With all these special features, bloodhounds can follow a scent all the way to the end of the trail.

Activity

TAKE A SENSE TEST **Try this classroom test to see if you can improve your mammalian senses. Put a blindfold on and then listen to sounds around you. Do you hear things you hadn't heard when you could see? Now have someone else give you an unidentified piece of fruit to eat while still blindfolded, but also while holding your nose. Does the fruit taste different when you can't see or smell it? Write down your observations from these experiments in your journal.**

SAVING
THE FLORIDA PANTHER

Florida, 1999

The Florida panther is in trouble. This majestic cat, the largest of its kind in the eastern United States, is on the brink of disappearing forever. Like hundreds of other mammals around the world, the Florida panther is an endangered species. As of this writing there are fewer than 60 of these animals left.

An animal may become endangered for a number of reasons. New human development and construction have drastically reduced the panther's habitat of forest and swamp. As its habitat shrinks, the panther has been forced to go into other areas to find food. Sometimes panthers cross highways and are killed by speeding cars and trucks. Others have been shot by hunters and farmers who mistakenly see them as a threat to humans. Pollution in the air and water has poisoned some panthers and made others ill. It has also damaged their immune system and made them more susceptible to disease.

What is the state of Florida doing to try to save the panther? In 1995, the state Fish and Wildlife Service (FWS) released eight Texas cougars into the panther's habitat. The cougar is one of the panther's closest relatives and experts hoped that the female cougars would breed with the male panthers and produce healthy young.

This kind of interbreeding has been going on among big cats and many other animals for a long, long time. Interbreeding expands the genetic pool and increases the chances that the offspring will be healthy and strong.

In 1996, three panther kittens were born. As other healthy kittens are born each year, the Florida panther's story looks more and more like it will have a happy ending. But for many other endangered mammals, the outcome is not so certain.

The Florida Panther at a Glance

DESCRIPTION: Member of cougar family, rust to gray coat, white on muzzle, chest, and underbelly

HABITAT: Upper dry lands and wetlands such as swamps and marshes

DIET: Deer, wild hogs, raccoons, small alligators, and rodents

SOCIAL BEHAVIOR: Males live alone, female care for young, most active at dusk and dawn when hunting

OUTSTANDING TRAITS: Can reach speed of 35 mph for short spurts, has keen sense of smell and vision, famous for panther scream

LIFE SPAN: 12–15 years in wild

Other Ways Florida Is Trying to Save the Panther

CAPTIVE BREEDING Ten panther kittens were removed from the wild in 1991 and 1992. In captivity, the kittens can be protected and cared for and eventually returned to the wild. Not entirely successful, this program has been recently put on hold.

RADIO TRACKING Most of the panthers were briefly captured and equipped with radio collars that give off electronic signals. These allow humans to track the panthers' movements. The information they receive about the panthers' behavior and lifestyle can be invaluable in trying to save them.

PARTNERSHIPS WITH PRIVATE LANDOWNERS While some panthers live on public lands, such as Everglades National Park, others range over private lands that are quickly being developed. The state has offered money and other economic incentives to private landowners to keep their land in a natural state so it can remain a habitat for the panther and other wild animals.

Call of the Wild

A growing number of people are enjoying jobs that involve wildlife. In the U.S., most work at the 500 government wildlife refuges, which allow animals to roam freely in areas specifically maintained for their needs. Many new careers center on coping with the effects of pollution and deforestation on wildlife.

Want to work outside? Consider work as an outdoor recreation planner. They coordinate the use of refuge land and waters, in addition to planning nature walks and visitor education programs.

Love law? A wildlife conservation officer enforces laws regarding hunting, trapping, and fishing. The officer patrols a district in search of law breakers, and assists in the prosecution of criminal charges against violators.

A growing field of concern is extinction. Biologists with the U.S. Fish and Wildlife Service help create recovery plans for the more than 700 plant and animal species in danger of dying out.

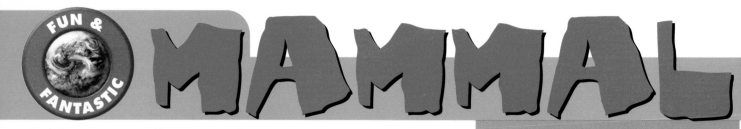

Bizarre and Beautiful Noses

Star-nosed mole—the nearly blind mammal uses its nose to ······▶ get around.

Elephant seal—the male elephant seal can inflate his nose to twice the size to frighten away enemies and catch the eye of the female.

Elephant—It's a nose, it's a hand, it's an arm—this versatile organ helps an elephant eat, drink, communicate and smell.

THE TOOTH OF THE MATTER

Walrus—The males use their tusks as weapons to battle each other for females. They also are used to hoist them out of the icy waters onto the ice.

Narwhal—The narwhal's teeth have adapted to become a long swordlike horn.

EARS TO YOU

Elephant—Biggest of the big, these jumbo flaps keep the elephant cool. They're good for communicating too. Flapping ears mean "Go away!"

Bat—Bats use sonar—high-pitched sounds— to find insects and make their way around in the dark. They send out high-pitched tones that bounce off objects and echo back. A bat's ears pick up the sounds.

Hare—Big ears keep this desert mammal cool by allowing heat to dissipate.

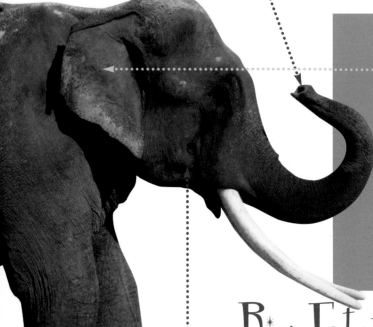

Big Eaters

- An adult giant anteater can consume 30,000 termites in a day.

- An average bat can devour 4,000 flying insects in a night.

- The common mole eats nearly its own weight in insects and worms every day.

- An elephant eats up to 50 tons of its grassy environment each year.

- A platypus can eat 1,400 earthworms, 50 fresh water crayfish, and 40 tadpoles in one night.

mania

The Truth About Mammals

- Many species of bats are vegetarians—or fruitarians. The bulk of the others eat insects. There are, however, a couple of species that feed on animals. The tiny vampire bat of Latin America makes a small incision in the udder of a cow, then laps up the blood with its tongue like a cat drinking milk. It rarely attacks humans.

- Pigs like to wallow in mud because it cools them off and protects them from the sun. A pig's skin is very sensitive and can sunburn easily.

- Outdoor laborers in India protect themselves from tiger attacks by wearing masks on the back of their heads. Tigers attack only from behind and will not attack a man that is "facing" them!

ED: What's worse than a GIRAFFE with a sore throat?

FRED: An ELEPHANT with a runny nose.

MISNAMED MAMMALS

The koala bear is not a bear but a marsupial.

The spiny anteater is not an anteater, although it does eat ants.

The sea cow is not a cow.

The maned wolf is actually a fox.

The flying fox is actually a bat.

The killer whale and pilot whale are both dolphins.

Q: What is a monkey's favorite month?
A: Ape-ril.

UNUSUAL NAMES FOR MAMMAL GROUPS

A CLOWDER OF CATS

A SKULK OF FOXES

A TROOP OF KANGAROOS

A MOB OR PRIDE OF LIONS

A LOOM OF GIRAFFES

A PLASH OF POLAR BEARS

A BUMBLE OF BEARS

A TRIP OF SEALS

A SUPERIORITY OF CAMELS

A TRIUMPH OF TIGERS

Final Project:
The Last Living Mammal

You've now read all about mammals. How far they've come … how they've adapted … their amazing diversity. And it's time to ask the question: What would the world be like without them?

Assume that there occurs a sudden major catastrophe—picking one from the list at right, or making up your own. Assume that whichever one you pick will result in the total destruction of all mammals except one species. Your job is to tell which species has survived. Is it the biggest, strongest, smallest, most intelligent? Just what critter will be the last mammal on Earth? Perhaps it's the one most like other classes of animals—insects, reptiles, fish, etc. Or maybe it's an animal we now consider a pest. Or, a marine mammal. What will these animals encounter in this post-apocalyptic world? What will be the effect of their offspring on the food chain? What habitats and ecosystems will they find? What adaptations might they undergo?

Write your findings in a special edition of a Martian colony newspaper, where a small colony of humans have taken refuge. Your headline should be, The Last Living Mammal, explaining what led up to the extinction of the rest of the mammals on earth—and what is predicted to happen next.

- ▶ The polar ice caps melt, flooding the earth's surface.

- ▶ An asteroid strikes the earth. Depending on its location—land, ocean, or one of the poles, the results would vary.

- ▶ A volcanic eruption blocks out the sun.

- ▶ Disease wipes out plant life.

- ▶ Famine or disease wipes out all orders of mammals but one, which is resistant.

Ready for the ultimate challenge?
Enter this or any other science project in the
Discovery Young Scientist Challenge.
Visit discoveryschool.com/dysc to find out how.